IDENTITY

6

s

Receiving Identity *from God*

[DALE &
JUANITA RYAN]

Letting God Be God Bible Studies

IVP

InterVarsity Press
Downers Grove, Illinois

InterVarsity Press
P.O. Box 1400, Downers Grove, IL 60515-1426
World Wide Web: www.ivpress.com
E-mail: mail@ivpress.com

InterVarsity Press® is the book-publishing division of InterVarsity Christian Fellowship/USA®, a student movement active on campus at hundreds of universities, colleges and schools of nursing in the United States of America, and a member movement of the International Fellowship of Evangelical Students. For information about local and regional activities, write Public Relations Dept., InterVarsity Christian Fellowship/USA, 6400 Schroeder Rd., P.O. Box 7895, Madison, WI 53707-7895.

Cover photograph: Michael Goss

Cover logo and interior icons: Roberta Polfus

ISBN 0-8308-2075-2

Printed in the United States of America ∞

19	18	17	16	15	14	13	12	11	10	9	8	7	6	5	4	3	2	1
16	15	14	13	12	11	10	09	08	07	06	05	04	03	02	01			

CONTENTS

INTRODUCTION: RECEIVING IDENTITY FROM GOD

Know that the LORD is God.
  It is he who made us, and we are his.
(Psalm 100:3)

Who am I? It is one of the most basic questions we ask in life. Most of us attempt, at one time or another, to answer this question in superficial ways. We may, at times, believe that we are what we do—or that we are what we have accomplished. We may, at times, believe that we are what we buy—that our identity comes from the stuff we own. At other times, we may believe that we are what we look like—that our identity comes from our body's size, shape and appearance. Or we may believe that we are who other people think we are. Or the various roles we play. Or that we are what happened to us. Sooner or later most of us come to believe—or at least suspect—that these kinds of answers to the question of our identity are not satisfying; they are not answers at all.

Christians have always believed that the answer to the question "Who am I?" lies not in our thoughts, behaviors, roles, appearance, intentions or possessions. The answer lies, rather, in the heart of God. Who we are is found in who God is. God is Creator. We are God's treasured creation. God is compassionate Father. We are God's much-loved children. An important part of "letting God be God" in our lives is to let God provide us with our core identity.

God offers us the wonderful gift of knowing who we are. God offers us a foundation of love and belonging—an identity in which we can rest securely, rich soil in which to grow. But we resist this gift. We even struggle against it. The gift seems too good to be true. We think we don't deserve to be loved and treasured and cared for by our Creator. We believe, instead, that we need to prove ourselves, that we need to make ourselves into something. This only leads to a sense of competition, comparison and separation from others, and to a sense of failure within because it seems we can never do enough or be enough. When we lose connection with God as our source of identity, our lives can become disordered, unmanageable and exhausting.

The gift of identity which God offers us may seem too good to be true, but as we receive God more fully into our lives, we also more deeply receive our true identity as God's precious creatures, God's dearly loved children. The studies in this guide are designed to help you open your heart and life to the God who made you and who knows who you are. It is our prayer that in the process of working through these studies God's Spirit will free you to receive God's gift of identity more fully.

Learning to Let God Be God

The Bible studies in this series are based on three basic convictions. The first of these convictions is that we are by our very nature dependent on our Maker. We need God. We need God's help with the daily challenges of life. We need God's love, peace, forgiveness, guidance and hope. The invitation to "let God be God" is an invitation to let God be who God really is. But it is also an invitation to us to be who we really are—God's deeply loved children.

Second, these studies are based on the conviction that God is willing, ready and eager to be God in our lives. God is not distant, inaccessible or indifferent. Rather, God is actively involved, offering us all that we need. God offers us all the love, strength, hope and peace we need.

Finally, these studies are based on the conviction that the spiritual life begins with receiving from God. What we do when we "let God be God" is receive from God the good gifts that God is eager to give to us. God has offered to love us. We are "letting God be God" when we receive this love. God has offered to guide us. We are "letting God be God" when we receive this guidance. Receiving from God is the starting point of the spiritual life. There is, of course, a place in the Christian journey for giving to God—a place for commitment and dedication. But if we have not learned well to receive from God, then we will almost certainly experience the Christian journey to be full of heavy burdens.

These are basic Christian convictions that closely resemble the first three steps of the twelve steps of Alcoholics Anonymous. The short summary is "I can't. God can. I'll let him." These are spiritual truths that apply to all of our lives. They may seem pretty simple. But most of us find that actually doing them—putting these truths into practice—is anything but simple. The problem is that receiving is not instinctive for most of us. What is instinctive is self-sufficiency, independence and managing by ourselves. What comes naturally is trying harder and trying our hardest. Letting go of this performance-oriented spirituality and allowing ourselves to receive from God will be a challenging adventure for most of us. It is the adventure that is at the heart of these Bible studies.

These Bible studies are designed to help you explore what it means to receive from God—what it means to let God be God in your life. George MacDonald used a wonderful metaphor when talking about the process of learning to receive from God. He said, "There are good things God must delay giving, until his child has a pocket to hold them—until God gets his child to make that pocket" (as cited in Michael R. Phillips, ed., *Discovering the Character of God* [Minneapolis: Bethany House, 1989], p. 156). These studies are designed to help you sew some new pockets that are big enough to hold the abundant good gifts that God has prepared for you.

Getting the Most from These Studies

The guides in this series are designed to assist you to find out what the Bible has to say about God and to grow in your ability to "let God be God" in your life. The passages you study will be thought provoking, challenging, inspiring and very personal. It will become obvious that these studies are not designed merely to convince you of the truthfulness of some idea. And they won't provide a systematic presentation of everything the Bible says about any subject. Rather, they will create an opportunity for biblical truths to renew your heart and mind.

There are six studies in each guide. Our hope is that this will provide you with maximum flexibility in how you use these guides. Combining the guides in various ways will allow you to adapt them to your time schedule and to focus on the concerns most important to you or your group.

All of the studies in this series use a workbook format. Space is provided for writing responses to each question. This is ideal for personal study and allows group members to prepare in advance for the discussion. The guides also contain notes with suggestions on how to lead a group discussion. The notes provide additional background information on certain questions, give helpful tips on group dynamics and suggest ways to deal with problems that may arise during the discussion. These features equip someone with little or no experience to lead an effective discussion.

Suggestions for Individual Study

1. As you begin each study, pray that God would give you wisdom and courage through his Word.

2. After spending time in preparation, read and reread the passage to be studied.

3. Write your responses in the space provided or in a personal journal. Writing can bring clarity and deeper understanding of yourself and God's Word. For the same reason, we suggest that you write out your prayers at various points in each study.

4. Most of the studies include questions that invite you to spend time in meditative prayer. The biblical text is communication addressed personally to us. Meditative prayer can enrich and deepen your experience of a biblical text.

5. After you have completed your study of the passage, you might want to read the leader's notes at the back of the guide to gain additional insight and information.

6. Share what you are learning with someone you trust. If you are not able to use these guides in a group you might want to consider participating in one of our online discussion groups at <www.lettinggodbegod.com>.

Suggestions for Group Study

Even if you have already done these studies individually, we strongly encourage you to find some way to do them with a group of other people as well. Although each person's journey is different, everyone's journey is empowered by the mutual support and encouragement that can only be found in a one-on-one or group setting. Several reminders may be helpful for participants in a group study.

1. Trust grows over time. If opening up in a group setting feels risky, realize that you do not have to share more than what feels safe to you. However, taking risks is a necessary part of growth. So do participate in the discussion as much as you are able.

2. Be sensitive to the other members of the group. Listen attentively when they talk. You will learn from their insights. If you can, link what you say to the comments of others so the group stays on the topic.

3. Be careful not to dominate the discussion. We are sometimes so eager to share what we have learned that we do not leave opportunity for others to respond. By all means participate! But allow others to do so as well.

4. Expect God to teach you through the passage being discussed and through the other members of the group. Pray that you will have a profitable time together.

5. We recommend that groups follow a few basic guidelines and that these guidelines be read at the beginning of each discussion session. The guidelines, which you may wish to adapt to your situation, are

☐ Anything said in the group is considered confidential and will not be discussed outside the group unless specific permission is given to do so.

☐ We will provide time for each person present to talk if he or she feels comfortable doing so.

☐ We will talk about ourselves and our own situations, avoiding conversation about other people.

☐ We will listen attentively to each other.

☐ We will be very cautious about giving advice.

☐ We will pray for each other.

If you are the discussion leader, you will find additional suggestions and helpful ideas for each study in the leader's notes. These are found at the back of the guide.

You might also want to consider participating in the online discussion forum for group leaders at <www.lettinggodbegod.com>.

1

Seeking Identity

PSALM 8

One of the problems with finding our identity is that we are works in process. We change at different rates—sometimes slowly and sometimes quickly—but we all change. This is a very good thing because when we lose the capacity for change we also lose our capacity for growth. But change can also be a frustrating thing. It can add to the sense of not knowing who we really are.

When our sense of identity is shifting, it helps to have some stable point of reference. A fixed point can help us gain perspective and give us a solid foundation to help us during times of change. According to Scripture, this stable point of reference is that we are the workmanship of a skilled and loving Creator. We are God's creation. The ways this fundamental truth can impact our lives are the focus of this study.

PREPARE
What do you hope to receive from these studies?

Let yourself answer the question "Who am I?" in as many ways as possible. List every possible answer to this question that comes to mind.

READ

¹*O LORD, our Lord,*
how majestic is your name in all the earth!
You have set your glory
above the heavens.
²*From the lips of children and infants*
you have ordained praise
because of your enemies,
to silence the foe and the avenger.

³*When I consider your heavens,*
the work of your fingers,
the moon and the stars,
which you have set in place,
⁴*what is man that you are mindful of him,*
the son of man that you care for him?
⁵*You made him a little lower than the heavenly beings*
and crowned him with glory and honor.

⁶*You made him ruler over the works of your hands;*
you put everything under his feet:
⁷*all flocks and herds,*
and the beasts of the field,
⁸*the birds of the air,*
and the fish of the sea,
all that swim the paths of the seas.

⁹*O LORD, our Lord,*
how majestic is your name in all the earth! (Psalm 8)

STUDY

1. This psalm is a song, a prayer, a poem, a heart cry. Where do you picture the psalmist sitting as he pens this psalm?

2. What does the psalmist say about God?

3. In verses 3 and 4 the psalmist contrasts himself with the vastness of creation and God's majesty. What kinds of feelings is the psalmist experiencing?

4. Describe a time when you felt this way.

5. How does this perspective compare with some of our culture's popular perspectives of what it means to be human?

6. How might sharing the perspective expressed by the psalmist's question in verses 3 and 4 impact the way we live?

7. What does the psalmist say in verses 5-8 about the identity and value that God has given humans?

8. In a time of quiet, reread the second half of verse 5, inserting your name in this phrase. Do this three or four times, allowing yourself to take this truth in as much as possible.

Write about your experience of reflecting on the text in this way.

9. In another time of quiet, picture yourself crowned "with glory and honor." Respond directly to God about this statement of who God made you to be.

Write about your experience in this time of prayer.

---

10. What conclusions would you draw from this text about your identity?

REFLECT
The psalmist understands the importance of both humility and honor. Both come from knowing we are the creatures of a loving Creator. Spend some time in quiet asking God to show you more about the truth and importance of both humility and honor.

RESPOND
Spend some time this week being in and reflecting on God's creation. Whether it is in your own backyard, in a park, or going hiking or camping. Spend some time looking, seeing, noticing and experiencing being a part of God's majestic creation. You may want to write about what you experience.

2

The Gift
of Identity

PSALM 139:1-18

The fundamental answer to the question "Who are we?" is "We are God's creatures." But there is more to the story than that. Since our identity comes from God, who we are is wrapped up in who God is.

If God is distant, then we are creatures abandoned and on our own. If God is cruel, then we are creatures hiding in fear. If God is impossible to please, then we are creatures perpetually despairing and exhausted.

But what if God is with us—loving us and watching over us? Then we are not abandoned but attended to, nurtured, provided for, never alone. What if God is kind and compassionate? Then we do not have to be afraid; we can rest in God's care for us. What if God delights in us? Then we can enjoy being close to God; we can be glad and full of joy, knowing we are God's much-loved children.

According to Scripture, God is with us always, God is compassionate and kind, and God delights in us. In the text for this study we will see, through the psalmist's eyes, the God who made us, who never leaves us, who cares for us and who delights in us.

PREPARE
What fears do you have about what God might say about your identity?

What hopes do you have about what God might say about your identity?

READ

¹*O LORD, you have searched me*
and you know me.
²*You know when I sit and when I rise;*
you perceive my thoughts from afar.
³*You discern my going out and my lying down;*
ou are familiar with all my ways.
⁴*Before a word is on my tongue*
you know it completely, O LORD.

⁵*You hem me in—behind and before;*
you have laid your hand upon me.
⁶*Such knowledge is too wonderful for me,*
too lofty for me to attain.

⁷*Where can I go from your Spirit?*
Where can I flee from your presence?
⁸*If I go up to the heavens, you are there;*
if I make my bed in the depths, you are there.
⁹*If I rise on the wings of the dawn,*
if I settle on the far side of the sea,
¹⁰*even there your hand will guide me,*
your right hand will hold me fast.

¹¹*If I say, "Surely the darkness will hide me*
and the light become night around me,"
¹²*even the darkness will not be dark to you;*
the night will shine like the day,
for darkness is as light to you.

¹³*For you created my inmost being;*
you knit me together in my mother's womb.
¹⁴*I praise you because I am fearfully and wonderfully made;*
your works are wonderful,
I know that full well.

[15]My frame was not hidden from you
    when I was made in the secret place.
When I was woven together in the depths of the earth,
[16] your eyes saw my unformed body.
All the days ordained for me
    were written in your book
    before one of them came to be.

[17]How precious to me are your thoughts, O God!
    How vast is the sum of them!
[18]Were I to count them,
    they would outnumber the grains of sand.
When I awake,
    I am still with you. (Psalm 139:1-18)

STUDY

1. What themes do you see in this text?

2. What does the psalmist say about God?

3. How does this description of God compare with your view of God?

4. Write an honest, personal response to what the psalmist says about God in this psalm.

5. How does the psalmist respond to God?

6. What does the psalmist say about himself?

7. If the psalmist were to make a statement about the identity he has received from God based on the reflections in this psalm, what might he say?

8. How does the psalmist's sense of identity compare with your own sense of identity?

9. What fears might keep you from seeing yourself in the way the psalmist saw himself?

10. What changes might it make (or has it made) in your life to see yourself as the psalmist sees himself?

11. In a time of quiet invite God to make you more aware of his loving presence with you. Allow yourself to relax in God's loving presence.

Write about your experience in this time of prayer.

REFLECT

Use verses 7-12 of this psalm as a prayer. Write whatever you sense God is showing you.

RESPOND

Spend some time each day this week rereading this text and repeating the prayer exercise in question 11. Write each day about your reflections.

3

Rejecting God's Gift of Identity

LUKE 15:1-7

God made us. God loves us. God says, "You are a creature of my making whom I treasure, a child whom I love and in whom I delight." This is who we are. This identity is God's gift to us.

For a variety of reasons, many of us find it very difficult to believe that God loves us faithfully, fully and unconditionally. Accepting an identity based on God's love can be particularly difficult if we have based our identity in the past on relationships in which we have not been loved faithfully, fully and unconditionally. A love like God's love may seem too good to be true. When we struggle with fears of this kind, we may find ourselves, consciously or unconsciously, rejecting the gift of identity that God offers to us. We may be hesitant, cautious or defensive about the thing we need most in life—to be loved by God.

When we resist God's gift of identity, we do not see ourselves through God's loving eyes; we lose connection with how precious and valuable we are. And when we resist God's gift of identity we may find ourselves treating others as if they do not deserve this gift either.

In the text for this study, Jesus tells a story to help us see ourselves through God's eyes.

PREPARE

What negative views are you aware of having about yourself?

What negative views are you aware of having about God?

READ

¹Now the tax collectors and "sinners" were all gathering around to hear him. ²But the Pharisees and the teachers of the law muttered, "This man welcomes sinners and eats with them."

³Then Jesus told them this parable: ⁴"Suppose one of you has a hundred sheep and loses one of them. Does he not leave the ninety-nine in the open country and go after the lost sheep until he finds it? ⁵And when he finds it, he joyfully puts it on his shoulders ⁶and goes home. Then he calls his friends and neighbors together and says, 'Rejoice with me; I have found my lost sheep.' ⁷I tell you that in the same way there will be more rejoicing in heaven over one sinner who repents than over ninety-nine righteous persons who do not need to repent. (Luke 15:1-7)

STUDY

1. There is a story within a story in this text. The first story is about the religious leaders (Pharisees and teachers of the law). The second story is the story Jesus told. What title would you give each story?

2. The Pharisees and teachers of the law (religious law) worked hard to do "what was right" and, as a result, saw themselves as spiritually superior to others. Think of an experience you have had with being on the receiving end of such arrogance and judgment. What impact did it have on you?

3. Think of a time that you have been the one doing the judging. What fear(s) led you to be judgmental?

4. What fears about God would fuel the kind of judgment the religious leaders were making?

5. What does this kind of judgment say about a person's sense of identity?

6. How does the story Jesus told speak to the religious leaders' fears about God?

7. What does Jesus' story communicate to the religious leaders about their sense of identity?

8. What impact would it have on you to see yourself as this treasured lamb?

9. What might make you hesitant to receive this identity?

---

10. In a time of quiet, reread Jesus' story in verses 4-6, putting yourself and your name in the story as the lamb who is lost.

Write about your responses to experiencing God and yourself in this way.

---

11. In another time of quiet picture yourself as the lamb in this story. Stay with this image and experience for a few minutes.

Write about your experience in this time of meditative prayer.

REFLECT

Read and reflect on the entire chapter of Luke 15. Put yourself in each story. Reflect on the description of God found in each story.

RESPOND

Each day this week, ask God to show you the fears about yourself or about God that might keep you from receiving God's gift of identity. And each day this week, use questions 10 and 11 to reflect on who you are and who God is. Write about what you sense God is showing you.

4

Being Open to God's Gift of Identity

MATTHEW 18:1-4

God wants us to know we are dearly loved children. God invites us to receive this gift of identity—this gift of love and belonging.

But in our pride and defensiveness we may be tempted to resist this gift. The truth is that our pride and defensiveness are nothing more than a cover-up for the fact that we are afraid. We are afraid that God is not truly loving. We are afraid that our identity is not a gift that God can give us, but is instead something that must be earned by thinking or doing all the right things. These fears lead us to jockey for positions and approval. They lead to competition and separation between us.

In the text for this study we will see that Jesus' disciples came to him in the midst of this kind of fearful jockeying. They did not know that they were afraid. They did not know how far off track they were. In this text we will see how Jesus gently and effectively invites them to let go of their fears. We will hear Jesus invite the disciples to become like little children again—to know themselves to be God's dearly loved children.

 PREPARE

List all the positive attributes of little children that you can think of.

READ

¹At that time the disciples came to Jesus and asked, "Who is the greatest in the kingdom of heaven?" ²He called a little child and had him stand among them. ³And he said: "I tell you the truth, unless you change and become like little children, you will never enter the kingdom of heaven. ⁴Therefore, whoever humbles himself like this child is the greatest in the kingdom of heaven." (Matthew 18:1-4)

STUDY

1. If you were a newspaper reporter and had the assignment of covering this story in fifty words or less, how would you write up the story?

2. What do you think was going on in the disciples' minds when they came to Jesus?

3. In what ways do you get caught up in similar anxieties?

4. Jesus responds to his disciples by telling them to change—to humble themselves and become like little children. What is Jesus saying to them?

5. What changes would result from this central shift in identity?

6. Why is this change necessary?

7. Put yourself in the disciples' place. What resistance would you feel to Jesus' invitation to change?

8. What is the attraction of this invitation?

9. What resistance and attraction do you feel in response to this invitation to humble yourself and become like a little child?

10. In a moment of quiet, see yourself as a trusting, loving child standing next to Jesus. Stay with this image for a few minutes, letting the gifts of this identity flow through you.

Write about your experience in this time of prayer.

REFLECT
Read and reflect on Romans 8:15-16.

Write about your thoughts and feelings in response to this text.

RESPOND
Use question 10 each day this week. Keep a daily journal of your experience with this prayer.

5

Receiving Identity from God

PSALM 103:1-14

God offers us identity. God offers us love and belonging. God reminds us that we are treasured creatures, dearly loved children.

We resist this offer of identity because of our fears about God and our fears about ourselves. These fears lead us into lives of trying hard, trying harder and trying our hardest—lives marked by exhaustion, discouragement and a sense of separation from God and others. But as we become aware of our fears and negative beliefs about ourselves and about God, we can ask God to heal these fears, and we can begin to open ourselves more deeply to receiving God's gift of identity. As we will see in this psalm, one key to the ongoing act of receiving from God is gratitude. As we express our thanks to God for who God is and for who we are, our hearts and minds take in the good gift of our true identity as God's much-loved children.

PREPARE

What fears come to mind when you think of the words *depend* and *dependent?*

What hopes and longings come to mind when you think of the words *depend* and *dependent?*

READ

¹Praise the LORD, O my soul;
*   all my inmost being, praise his holy name.*
²Praise the LORD, O my soul,
and forget not all his benefits—
³who forgives all your sins
*   and heals all your diseases,*
⁴who redeems your life from the pit
*   and crowns you with love and compassion,*
⁵who satisfies your desires with good things
*   so that your youth is renewed like the eagle's.*

⁶The LORD works righteousness
*   and justice for all the oppressed.*

⁷He made known his ways to Moses,
*   his deeds to the people of Israel:*
⁸The LORD is compassionate and gracious,
*   slow to anger, abounding in love.*
⁹He will not always accuse,
*   nor will he harbor his anger forever;*
¹⁰He does not treat us as our sins deserve
*   or repay us according to our iniquities.*
¹¹For as high as the heavens are above the earth,
*   so great is his love for those who fear him;*
¹²as far as the east is from the west,
*   so far has he removed our transgressions from us.*
¹³As a father has compassion on his children,
*   so the LORD has compassion on those who fear him;*
¹⁴for he knows how we are formed,
*   he remembers that we are dust. (Psalm 103:1-14)*

STUDY

1. What themes do you see in this psalm?

2. Make a list of the many loving actions this psalm says God does on our behalf.

3. What does the psalm say about who God is?

4. How does the description of God in this psalm compare to your expectations of God on a daily basis?

5. What does this psalm say about who we are?

6. What negative reactions do you have to this identity?

7. What positive reactions do you have to this identity?

8. In a time of quiet, reread the list of God's loving actions. Personalize these actions as you read by picturing God taking each action on your behalf.

Write about your experience in this time of meditative prayer.

9. In another time of quiet, invite God to give you new eyes to see yourself as God's dearly loved child whom God actively nurtures and loves.

Write about your experience in this time of prayer.

---

10. Write a prayer, expressing your thanks to God for who God is and for who you are.

REFLECT

Read Micah 6:8 several times. Ask God to show you what it would mean for you to walk humbly as God's dearly loved child. Write about whatever comes to you in this time of reflection.

RESPOND

Spend some time each day this week using the meditative prayer in question 8. Keep a journal of your experience each day as you pray in this way.

6

Celebrating Our Identity

PSALM 100

"Shout for joy to the LORD. . . . Worship the LORD with gladness."

This powerful invitation is found in Psalm 100. Why? Why all this joy and gladness toward God? Because God is the Lord who is good and whose love endures forever. Because God made us. Because we belong to God. When we know who God is and who we are, there is much to be glad about.

When we know that we are creatures—that we are not God—we do not have to assume God's responsibilities! When we know that we are dearly loved children of a compassionate God, we can live free of fears that we are not good enough or that we will be rejected. When we know that we belong to God and that God's goodness and love can be trusted, we can romp like lambs just let out to pasture.

PREPARE
Take three minutes and make a list of all the things you are grateful for at this moment. Write whatever comes to mind.

READ

¹*Shout for joy to the LORD, all the earth.*
² *Worship the LORD with gladness;*
   come before him with joyful songs.
³*Know that the LORD is God.*
   It is he who made us, and we are his;
   we are his people, the sheep of his pasture.
⁴*Enter his gates with thanksgiving*
   and his courts with praise;
   give thanks to him and praise his name.
⁵*For the LORD is good and his love endures forever;*
   his faithfulness continues through all generations. (Psalm 100)

STUDY

1. Think about a time when you were filled with joy and gratitude toward God. Tell about your experience.

---

2. What does the psalmist invite us to remember about God?

---

3. What does he invite us to remember about who we are?

4. The psalm is one of joy and gladness. What about our identity as God's creatures leads to joy and gladness?

5. What perspective have you gained (or renewed) about your identity in the past weeks of doing this study?

6. What impact has this had on your life?

7. In a moment of quiet, ask God to show you the false beliefs that you have had about who you are. Write about what you sense God is showing you. On a separate piece of paper write out these false identities. You might want to symbolize you release of these false identities by tearing the paper and throwing it away.

8. Write a statement about who God is from your own experience.

9. Write a statement about who you are.

10. Write your own prayer of joy and gratitude to God.

REFLECT
Reread the text from these six studies that had the most impact on you. Spend some time reflecting on it again.

RESPOND
Read what you wrote in response to questions 8, 9 and 10 each day this week. Keep this where you will see it often. Thank God each day for who you are and for who God is.

LEADER'S NOTES

You may be experiencing a variety of feelings as you anticipate leading a group through this study guide. You may feel inadequate for the task and afraid of what will happen. If this is the case, know you are in good company. Many other small group leaders share this experience. It may help you to know that your willingness to lead is a gift to the other group members. It might also help if you tell them about your feelings and ask them to pray for you. Realize as well that the other group members share the responsibility for the group. And realize that it is the Spirit's work to bring insight, comfort, healing and recovery to group members. Your role is simply to provide guidance to the discussion. The suggestions listed below will help you to provide that guidance.

Preparing to Lead

1. Develop realistic expectations of yourself as a small group leader. Do not feel that you have to "have it all together." Rather, commit yourself to an ongoing discipline of honesty about your own needs. As you grow in honesty about your own needs, you will grow as well in your capacity for compassion, gentleness and patience with yourself and with others. As a leader you can encourage an atmosphere of honesty by being honest about yourself.

2. Pray. Pray for yourself. Pray for the group members. Invite the Spirit to be present as you prepare and as you meet.

3. Read the text several times.

4. Take your time to thoughtfully work through each question, writing out your answers.

5. After completing your personal study, read through the leader's notes for the study you are leading. These notes are designed to help you in several ways. First, they tell you the purpose the authors had in mind while writing the study. Take time to think through how the questions work together to accomplish that purpose. Second, the notes provide you with additional background information or comments on some of the questions. This information can be useful when people have difficulty understanding or answering a question. Third, the leader's notes can alert you to potential problems you may encounter during the study.

6. If you wish to remind yourself during the group discussion of anything mentioned in the leader's notes, make a note to yourself below that question in your study guide.

Leading the Study

1. Begin on time. You may want to open in prayer, or have a group member do so.

2. Be sure everyone has a study guide. Decide as a group whether you want people to do the study on their own ahead of time. If your time together is limited, it will be helpful for people to prepare in advance.

3. At the beginning of your first time together, explain that these studies are meant to be discussions, not lectures. Encourage the members of the group to participate. However, do not put pressure on those who may be hesitant to speak during the first few sessions. Clearly state that people do not need to share anything they do not feel safe sharing. Remind people that it will take time to trust each other.

4. Read aloud the group guidelines listed in the front of the guide. These commitments are important in creating a safe place for people to talk and trust and feel.

5. Read aloud the introductory paragraphs at the beginning of the discussion for the day. This will orient the group to the passage being studied.

6. If the group does not prepare in advance, approximately ten minutes will be needed for individuals to work on the "Prepare" section. This is designed to help group members focus on some aspect of their personal experience. Hopefully it will help group members to be more aware of the frame of reference and life experience that we bring to the text. This time of personal reflection can be done prior to the group meeting or as the first part of the meeting. The prepare questions are not designed to be for group discussion, but you might begin by asking the group what they learned from the prepare questions.

7. Read the passage aloud. You may choose to do this yourself, or someone else may read if he or she has been asked to do so prior to the study.

8. As you begin to ask the questions in the guide, keep several things in mind. First, the questions are designed to be used just as they are written. If you wish, you may simply read them aloud to the group. Or you may prefer to express them in your own words. However, unnecessary rewording of the questions is not recommended.

Second, the questions are intended to guide the group toward under-standing and applying the main idea of the study. The authors of the guide have stated the purpose of each study in the leader's notes. You should try to understand how the study questions and the biblical text work together to lead the group in that direction.

There may be times when it is appropriate to deviate from the study guide. For example, a question may have already been answered. If so, move on to the next question. Or someone may raise an important question not covered in the guide. Take time to discuss it! The important thing is to use discretion. There may be many routes you can travel to reach the goal of the study. But the easiest route is usually the one the authors have suggested.

9. Don't be afraid of silence. People need time to think about the question before formulating their answers.

10. Don't be content with just one response. Ask, "What do the rest of you think?" or "Anything else?" until several people have given answers to the question.

11. Acknowledge all contributions. Try to be affirming whenever possible. Never reject an answer. If it seems clearly wrong to you, ask: "Which part of the text led you to that conclusion?" or "What do the rest of you think?"

12. Don't expect every answer to be addressed to you, even though this will probably happen at first. As group members become more at ease, they will begin to interact more effectively with each other. This is a sign of a healthy discussion.

13. Don't be afraid of controversy. It can be very stimulating. Differences can enrich our lives. If you don't resolve an issue completely, don't be frus-trated. Move on and keep it in mind for later. A subsequent study may resolve the problem.

14. Stick to the passage under consideration. It should be the source for answering the questions. Discourage the group from unnecessary cross-refer-encing. Likewise, stick to the subject and avoid going off on tangents.

15. Periodically summarize what the group has said about the topic. This helps to draw together the various ideas mentioned and gives continuity to the study. But be careful not to use summary statements as an opportunity to give a sermon!

16. End each study with a prayer time. You will want to draw on the themes of your study and individual prayer and meditation as you now pray together. There are several ways to handle this time in a group. The person who leads each study could lead the group in a prayer, or you could allow time for group participation. Remember that some members of your group may feel uncomfortable about participating in public prayer. It might be helpful to discuss this with the group during your first meeting and to reach some agreement about how to proceed.

Listening to Emotional Pain

These Bible study guides are designed to take seriously the pain and struggle that is part of life. People will experience a variety of emotions during these studies. Part of your role as group leader will be to listen to emotional pain. Listening is a gift that you can give to a person who is hurting. For many people it is not an easy gift to give. The following suggestions will help you to listen more effectively to people in emotional pain.

1. Remember that you are not responsible to take the pain away. People in helping relationships often feel that they are being asked to make the other person feel better. This is usually related to the helper's own anxiety about painful feelings.

2. Not only are you not responsible to take the pain away, but one of the things people need most is an opportunity to face and to experience the pain in their life. They may have spent years denying their pain and running from it. Healing can come when we are able to face our pain in the presence of someone who cares about us. Rather than trying to take the pain away, then, commit yourself to listening attentively as it is expressed.

3. Realize that some group members may not feel comfortable with others' expressions of sadness or anger. You may want to acknowledge that such emotions are uncomfortable but that part of the growth process is to learn to feel and allow others to feel.

4. Be very cautious about giving answers and advice. Advice and answers may make you feel better or competent, but they may also minimize peoples' problems and their painful feelings. Simple solutions rarely work, and they can easily communicate "You should be better now" or "You shouldn't really be talking about this."

5. Be sure to communicate direct affirmation any time people talk about their painful emotions. It takes courage to talk about our pain because it creates anxiety for us. It is a great gift to be trusted by those who are struggling.

Study Notes

The following notes refer to the questions in the Bible study portion of each study.

Study 1. Seeking Identity. Psalm 8.

Purpose: To join the psalmist in asking God, "Who am I?"

Question 1. The purpose of this question is to help participants get involved with the text. A variety of ideas can be expected.

Question 2. The psalmist talks about God's majesty and glory. He talks about God's creative power as Creator of the heavens and the earth. He acknowledges God as his Creator and as the One who has crowned him with glory and honor.

Question 3. Imagine the psalmist sitting outside on a starry night, in awe of the vastness of the sky. Perhaps the psalmist has spent the past several weeks camping out with the sheep, walking with them through valleys and over hillsides. The psalmist is deeply aware of God's creative glory, our smallness as creatures and God's vastness as Creator of all that is. He is feeling awe and wonder

Question 4. Encourage participants to remember a time when they felt awe and wonder, when they were particularly struck with God's creative power and with their place in the universe as one small creature.

Questions 5-6. Modern Western culture tends to see humans as the center of all things. We have lost much of this sense of humility as creatures of a majestic Creator. As a result, we strive for self-sufficiency and individuality, and tend to devalue our true dependency as creatures and our longing for deep connection with our Creator and each other. Returning to an awareness of ourselves as creatures could restore our capacity to depend on the One who made us and to seek God's guidance and help in all of life.

Question 7. The psalmist says that God has crowned us with glory and honor. This is a powerful reality to take in. The psalmist also talks about humans as being "a little lower than the heavenly beings" and about humans being given the power and responsibility to serve as rulers over all other life on earth.

Question 8. This would read, "You, oh God, have crowned me, [insert your name], with glory and honor."

Question 9. Participants may have a variety of responses to this statement. Most of us have some difficulty in fully comprehending the glory and honor that God gives us. We are not accustomed to the reality of God's deep valuing of us. We are not used to accepting the identity God gives us as creatures—of being crowned with glory and honor. Notice the absence of any conditional clauses here. There is no way to earn this or to become worthy of this. It is a part of who we are as God's creatures.

Allow participants time to pray and reflect alone. Invite any who want to share their experience in these times of quiet to do so.

Question 10. We are creatures. We are the creation of a majestic Creator. We are one small part of God's vast creation. Yet we are valued deeply by our Creator. God crowns us with glory and honor.

Study 2. The Gift of Identity. Psalm 139:1-18.

Purpose: To explore who we are as God's creation.

Question 1. The purpose of this question is to get an overview of the text. The themes present in this text all have to do with God's close, constant presence with us.

Question 2. The psalmist says that God knows him intimately, pays attention to him, is with him always and everywhere, guides him and protects him and holds onto him. The psalmist says that God created him, formed him, watched over him, and gave him the gift of each and every day of life.

Question 3. We sometimes think of God as distant, far away from us, rather than constantly close. Participants may find these statements about God's intimate involvement in their lives are very different from their view of God. Some may find it matches their view of God rather closely. Allow people to compare and contrast their views with those of this text in an honest way. As group leader, you may want to be prepared to share honestly and briefly any way this text surprised you or challenged your view of God.

Question 4. Responses may range from gratitude, to disbelief, to feeling afraid. Some people may have difficulty believing that God is this present with them. Some may feel they have to earn such attention and care. Some may fear that if God pays attention God will use any information collected to judge them. Some may have a growing sense of the truth of these statements about God and may see these truths as good news about God's intimate, ever present love for them.

Question 5. The psalmist responds with gratitude, joy and wonder at God's intimate involvement in his life.

Question 6. The psalmist says that he is fearfully and wonderfully made. He says that it is not possible to be separated from God, no matter where he goes. The psalmist acknowledges that he is a creature, created by a caring and wonderful Creator.

Question 7. The psalmist might say, "I am a created being, created by the Creator God who has been and always will be with me to guide me and help me."

Question 8. Encourage participants to be honest with their comparisons. Again, you might want to begin this discussion by sharing honestly and briefly about your own struggles to see yourself in the way this text describes.

Question 9. People may fear that they have to earn this kind of loving attention from God by being perfect or by jumping through certain religious hoops. Or they may be afraid that they are not lovable enough or valuable enough to deserve this kind of love and care.

Question 10. It can be profoundly transforming to see ourselves as God's creatures, to know that God is intimately present with us always, to know that God values us and cares for us deeply. This gift of identity from God can free us from needing to prove anything; it can free us to trust and rest in God's care.

Question 11. Allow participants time alone to be aware of God's presence with them. Invite participants who want to share to talk about their experience in this time of prayer.

Study 3. Rejecting God's Gift of Identity. Luke 15:1-7.

Purpose: To identify the ways we reject God's gift of identity.

Question 1. The purpose of this question is to get an overview of the text. Encourage a variety of responses.

Question 2. Being on the receiving end of judgment is painful and damaging. We feel separated from others, rejected, devalued.

Question 3. Judgment of others often comes out of fears about ourselves—that we are not good enough in some way.

Question 4. Judgment of others, especially spiritual judgments, are often fueled by fears that God is a harsh taskmaster, that God demands we do certain things or think certain thoughts before we can be accepted.

Question 5. The point here is that this kind of judgment comes from a negative view of oneself and a negative view of God. A person's identity in this case is rooted in fear of rejection rather than in the certainty of love.

Question 6. God is pictured in this story as a person who has lost a sheep. God is the one who loves and values that one lost sheep so deeply that he goes out in search of the sheep. This is not a story about economics. It was not profit that motivated the shepherd. The shepherd is strongly attached and deeply committed in love to the lost sheep. In this story, God is not harsh or demanding in any way. God is committed to us, God reaches out to us, God does not shame us for getting lost but is full of joy when we are found. God carries us in his arms and throws a party for us because we are of such value.

Question 7. Jesus' story is a powerful, tender story about God's love and the value of each and every person, including the people the religious leaders wanted to judge and condemn. Jesus is making the point that we are all God's sheep. We are all valued in this same way by God. We are God's own creatures, treasured and loved by God. This is our true identity.

Question 8. This identity, as a lamb—loved, lost, sought for, found, carried in joy, celebrated—might be seen as healing and freeing.

Question 9. For some, there may be a sense that God's unconditional love and valuing is too good to be true. The fears that we are not deserving, or that we have to earn or prove our worth run very deep in most of us.

Question 10. Give participants time alone to read and reflect on this text in this personal way. Invite people to share their experiences during this time of reflection, as they feel free to do so.

Study 4. Being Open to God's Gift of Identity. Matthew 18:1-4.

Purpose: To hear Jesus' invitation to receive our identity as God's children.

Question 1. Encourage a variety of responses to this question.

Question 2. The disciples are engaged in a conflict that is familiar to all of us. Who is the best? How do we know who is the best? What do I have to do to be seen by God as better than the next guy? How do I win at this competition? I don't want to be last. I don't want to be left out. I don't want anybody to be better than me.

This conflict inside us comes from our fears and insecurities. We do not think we can be loved and valued without somehow proving ourselves and earning our love and value. But what kind of love and value would it be if we had to earn it? What kind of love and value would it be if any one of us is ever more loved or more valued than the other? The love and value we receive from God is not conditional, not competitive, not possible to earn or to lose. It is constant, steadfast, intrinsic and all-inclusive.

Question 3. Encourage people to identify similar anxieties and insecurities in their own lives and to be as specific with examples as they can. As group leader you might want to be prepared with personal examples of how you experience this in order to share briefly with the group.

Question 4. Little children are unashamed of their needs. They are openly dependent on others. They entrust themselves to others' care. They seek the love of their caretakers and know that they have all they need when they are loved and valued. Little children need love and care, and they seek love and care. They readily trust a loving, trustworthy caretaker.

Question 5. The disciples are asking, "Who is greatest in the kingdom of heaven?" Jesus says, "Whoever humbles himself and becomes like a little child is greatest in the kingdom of heaven." The shift here is moving from doing and proving and competing—all out of fear of not being loved and accepted—to acknowledging our dependency on God and trusting that we are loved and accepted.

This central shift would lead to a decrease in stress and tension. It would relieve our deepest fear and anxiety. It would free us to relax, to rest securely in God's love. It would free us to live and love with energy, honesty, creativity and joy. It would keep us from separating ourselves from each other with judgment and competition.

Question 6. This change is necessary because it transforms our lives from lives lived in fear to lives lived in the security of God's loving arms. We are free, we are whole, we are able to be who God made us to be—his dearly loved children.

Question 7. The resistance the disciples might have felt is the same as our own. We have a difficult time giving up our fears and our attempts to earn our value. It seems too good to be true that in God's eyes our value is a given, and we are loved unconditionally.

Question 8. The attraction of the invitation is that it is so freeing. We do not have to worry about winning or losing. We already have what we want—we have God's full, constant, faithful love for us personally. We can trust this. We can rest in this. We can celebrate this and be glad.

Question 9. Encourage participants to be as specific and honest as they can. You might want to give the group a couple of minutes for private reflection about their thoughts and feelings in response to Jesus' statements in this text.

Question 10. Allow participants at least five minutes alone to pray and reflect in this way. Invite them to share anything they feel free to share from their time of prayer.

Study 5. Receiving Identity from God. Psalm 103:1-14.

Purpose: To open our hearts and minds to receive God's gift of identity.

Question 1. The psalmist is reminding himself in this psalm of who God is and of all God does on his behalf.

Question 2. God forgives our sins; God heals our diseases; God redeems our life from the pit; God crowns us with love and compassion; God satisfies our desires with good things; God renews our youth; God works righteousness and justice for all the oppressed; God makes his ways known to us; God loves us with a very, very great love; God removes our sins; God has compassion on us.

Question 3. The psalmist tells us that God is forgiver, healer, redeemer, one who crowns us, satisfier of our desires, life giver, helper of the oppressed, compassionate Father.

Question 4. Encourage participants to reflect on their expectations of God in the day-to-day realities of life. We often forget these truths about God. Like the psalmist, we would do well to remind ourselves each day about who God is, about God's active love for us at all times.

Question 5. This psalm reminds us that we are dust—we are mortal creatures. It reminds us that we are creatures in need of forgiveness and healing and redemption and help of every kind. This psalm also reminds us that we are loved by a God of love. More than anything else, we are children of a loving Creator.

Question 6. Encourage people to be honest about any negative reactions they may have to their mortality or their needs. We struggle with these realities all the time as humans.

Question 7. Encourage participants to respond from their hearts about what it feels like to be so loved.

Question 8. This time of prayer focuses primarily on God and on God's actions toward us individually.

Question 9. This time of prayer focuses primarily on us as individuals, and on how God sees us as God looks at us through eyes of love and delight and compassion. Allow participants time alone for questions 8 and 9. Invite any who want to share to talk about their experience while praying in this way.

Study 6. Celebrating Our Identity. Psalm 100.

Purpose: To find joy and freedom in our true identity.

Question 1. Encourage participants to share personal experiences of joy and gratitude toward God.

Question 2. The psalmist reminds us that God is the one who made us. He reminds us that God is good, that God's love endures forever, that God's faithfulness (commitment in love toward us) continues through all generations.

Question 3. The psalmist reminds us that we are God's creatures, God's people, the sheep of God's pasture.

Question 4. Because God is good, loving and trustworthy, and because God is God and we are not, we can be at peace. We do not need to be afraid. We can be free to enjoy the pasture.

Questions 5-6. Encourage people to share honestly about what they have learned as a result of these studies and their times of reflection and prayer. You might want to be prepared to share honestly and briefly some of your own experience.

Question 7. Give participants a few minutes to reflect and pray. You might want to lead the group in writing about their false identities and tearing up the pages and throwing them away.

Questions 8-10. Again, give participants time to reflect and write. It could be a moving time to share these reflections and writings with each other as a way of closing this study together.

Online Resources

If you would like to share your experience using this Bible study with other people, we invite you to join us online at

<www.lettinggodbegod.com>

At the website you will be able to sign up to receive a free daily meditation written by Dale and Juanita Ryan.

Additional resources of interest to some users of these studies can be found at the online home of the Ryans:

<www.christianrecovery.com>